T0143994

I Imagine

Sherry Richardson

Balboa Press books may be ordered through booksellers or by contacting:

Balboa Press
A Division of Hay House
1663 Liberty Drive
Bloomington, IN 47403
www.balboapress.com
1 (877) 407-4847

ISBN: 978-1-9822-0748-9 (sc)
978-1-9822-0747-2 (e)

Print information available on the last page.

Balboa Press rev. date: 07/05/2018

BALBOA
PRESS
A DIVISION OF HAY HOUSE

Table of Contents

Dedication

This book is lovingly dedicated to my sweet husband, Ron, who has passed and helps me constantly from the non-physical realm. Without his continual encouragement, gentle persuasion and unconditional Love, this book would have never been.

To my beautiful daughters Brenda and Carie, who have been my teachers since the day they were born.

Acknowledgements

With love and gratitude to Jo, who spent endless hours helping me with the research and details of publishing this book, all the while sharing her enthusiasm, joy and excitement as we journeyed together in this magnificent endeavor.

A very special thank you to my family members who have always been there for me and have always welcomed me to be who I Am.

With great appreciation and gratitude to Claire and John for their unconditional love and support during a dark period of my life.

I wish to thank all of my wonderful friends who have inspired, supported and loved me, not just during the publication of this book, but throughout my Journey of Life. You know who you are and I bless each and every one of you for being such an important and integral part of my life.

Enormous gratitude to all the artists who have contributed their beautiful artwork! I can't say enough about these wonderful artists - so talented and giving. The combination of artists extends all around the world - 13 countries in all. I have included each artist's contact information in the back of the book.

Introduction

This book contains material that allows the reader the opportunity to perceive reality in a different way.

The purpose of this book is to help release old thoughts and beliefs that keeps one repeating patterns of unwanted experiences. It is designed to assist the reader to connect with the Inner Nature of Self, a connection where True, Unconditional Love is always flowing.

The quotes have been birthed as inspiration to provide a moving experience into Alignment, therefore creating an allowing State of Being.

A Heart That is Open

Artist: Erica Wexler

A Heart That is Open Knows Worlds Beyond Description

A Heart that is open draws unto ItSelf desires that are fulfilled in physical form. When it manifests, another chance to expand the feeling is met, invoking more desires which creates Eternal Life.

There is a longing deep within your wandering Soul. It's calling you to remember your wholeness.

All is Good in the World

Artist: Daniel B. Holeman

All is Good in My World Because All is Good With Me

Projections out into the physical world will currently show what's active in one's vibration. Setting a well-being vibrational pattern first thing in the morning allows one to be the conscious co-creator they were meant to be. A true "Master" is one that is conscious of the unconscious.

Always Moving Toward Becoming

Artist: Anto Machado

I Will Hold MySelf to a Standard of GRACE, Not Perfection

I Am always moving toward becoming. Every choice I make contains an idea, which when focused on, creates a different version of me. Within this process I acknowledge *I Am That Which I Am.*

Animal Spirit Guides

Artist: Shirley D. Cross Taylor

I Call Upon My Animal Spirit Guides So That I May
See Their Essence to Help Light the Way of My Journey

The non-physical guides, the wayshowers, are closer to you than the breath. They appear in all forms. Listen closely to what animals you are pulled to, for they are your *Sacred Animal Guides* teaching you the attributes of their Beingness to guide you on your journey.

Birth to Self

Artist: Misticos Online

You Are Born to Give Birth to YourSelf

You are a vibrational Being, constantly creating from *frequency imaging*, which in the physical world is called manifesting. In the silence of BEing, there is no "urge" to be anything except who you are.

9

Conversation With Your Heart

Artist: Shirley D. Cross-Taylor

Sometimes you just have to sit outside and have a conversation with Your Heart. Nature will teach you what real prayer is: *To Embrace Life.*

Dear Self

Artist: Shirley D. Cross-Taylor

Wisdom is acknowledging YOUR nature, YOUR beliefs,
YOUR story. Letting go of the beliefs of others,
that at one time you accepted as your own

Dear Self,

   To be true to MySelf, I Am willing to rewrite the story of my journey from moment to moment. I vow to uphold in my actions and words the Divine Thoughts that come from my *Inner Being*, which exclude any beliefs.

Dream

Artist: Ed Hooijmans

Magic is Found Within a Dream, That is Within Another Dream, That is Dreaming of Endless Dreams

By embracing dreams, one rises to the highest potentials and opens doors to the experience of Oneness.

Therefore, I dream knowing the Dreamer is dreaming me.

Fear of Change

Artist: Erica Wexler

Fear of Change is the Ego's Altering of Its Illusionary Nature to Keep You From Knowing the Truth About Who YOU Really Are

When the realization is known of the underlying reason of fear, it usually is due to a belief that was imprinted in the physical body from birth. As the physical journey continued with the vibration of fear active, the belief was imprinted again and again, drawing in more experiences to "validate" from the ego's perspective making the illusion appear as real. The ego, being from the lower mind has an important part to play and that is to "perceive" what has happened. It should have no other responsibility than that. When more and more responsibilities are given to the ego, the ego will always be fearful, because it cannot solve problems, it cannot create desires and it certainly cannot give peace. When united with the Higher Mind, the vibration of fear dissipates and the ego now resonates in a higher state, which is Love. Then, and only then, can it work in unison to restore balance on all levels.

Freedom

Artist: Achraf Baznani

Freedom Comes the Moment We Realize There Were Never Any Answers - ONLY STORIES. The Ones who experience the whole story, are the Ones who step out of each book to write the next one.

Hocus Pocus

Artist: Ed Hooijmans

The Clues to Create
Are Found in the Words We Use

A brilliantly designed language was set forth by others before us to be used to co-create/manifest in this physical reality. If paid attention to, the "hidden" meaning reveals all that is necessary to create, reflect, understand and know what Powerful Beings we are.

The true meaning of "Hocus Pocus" is not "hidden" to the initiate who remembers the power of focusing on what is desired. Focus Focus is the power to create, to bring forth energy into form. That is where the magic is.

I Am Feeling Joy

Artist: Koh Sangwoo

I Am Feeling Joy Because
I Choose to Believe it's My Nature and Who I Truly Am

By stating "I Choose" or "I Prefer", a feeling of freedom empowers an individual. How often does one feel there is no choice? Once the Truth is established of always having a choice, one will allow the energy to activate different ideas or different ways of looking at situations. It "completes" the circuit that the mind has been running on a loop. There is a peace that settles in on all levels.

In the World in Which I Travel

Artist: Daniel B. Holeman

In the World in Which I Travel,
I Am Endlessly Creating MySelf.

Inspiration

Artist: Alla Tsyplakova - AkuBakaArts

Pay attention to what Inspires you, for It is Your Spirit in communication with you, sending you impulses of creative guidance, ideas and solutions. Life is given to what is held precious.

Listen to It, Believe It and Act on It

Into the Mystic

Artist: AdoreLuna

Into the Mystic...
  Embraced by Imagination...
    It is There I Choose to Live.

I Imagine, Because It is There I Find My Connection to Love.

Journey of the Soul

Artist: Achraf Baznani

In the journey of the Soul, the Higher Mind created a version of "you" by the beliefs vibrationally imprinted in the physical body from the illusion of being separate from "Self". Eventually, the incorporation of beliefs defining "you" became more active in your vibrational Being". Beliefs that were reflected in your outside world manifested as an illusion of "unworthiness", non-value and being unloved. This process made those beliefs seem real, as more manifestations entered the physical realm. When the "Awakening" started, the "Remembering" began. Within the "remembering", no belief systems of separation exist. The experiences of the journey, within the framework of the illusion of separation, created this physical reality to expand the Soul and in turn, expand All That Is. Each choice is a piece of the puzzle to represent the Whole.

Just Be Yourself

Artist: Benedigital aka Ben Encarnacion

Each of Us Has a Unique and Individual Energy Template Created by the One. That is Who We Are – How Can We Be Anything But That?

"Just Be Yourself." This quote is often stated over and over in the physical realm. As the mind desires the knowledge of the meaning, Spirit presents the impulse of meaning through a feeling that flows within the whole Self. At that exact moment the knowing of Being an individual expression of The One, with the full potential of Love, Joy, Fun, Compassion, Peace, Fulfillment and Passion that is expressed in the only way YOU can express it. No other Being can express those qualities of Spirit like YOU can, in your own special way that is Divinely and Uniquely YOU.

Karma is Self Image

Artist: Mariusz Lewandowski

When the Initiate comes to fully understand Self, there is no more denial of Truth. For Truth to the Initiate now reveals ItSelf with the meaning of karma, given from the Higher Self. Now seen from the meaning given by the Frequency of Love, how one sees Self is the energy put forth to create that manifestation in the physical realm. For to see Self in any limited way, is to draw upon one's Self the idea of that meaning, which manifests limitation seen from the physical eyes. That meaning is given when focused outside of Self. Therefore, drawing unto itself circumstances that appear to be a "punishment" or "reward". When seen through the eyes of Spirit, the manifestation drawn from that level of sight will always draw love, abundance and well being to the one focused on seeing Self from <u>no</u> belief system. Pay attention to Self talk - for that is where the power is. One is always one thought away from the illusion of separation.

Language of Love

Artist: Shirley D. Cross-Taylor

Communicating in Nature is Understanding the Language of Love

If there ever is any doubt what a powerful Being You are, look at what you've created - a physical reality that has the *illusion* of being separate from All That Is.

Thank you Mother Earth for the fun playground to play Hide & Seek with one another!

Living in Grace

Artist: Erica Wexler

The Gift of Living in Grace is Helping Others Open Doors

Defining one as "graceful" is a powerful acknowledgment of witnessing one moving about in Grace. It is Divinity in motion that captures the human eye and speaks to the physical self, calling attention to a moment in time referred to as *"Gracefull"*. This is the greatest gift one can give, for it requires no words. It is the movement of Spirit that draws another into the door of experiencing one's own Self as *"Full of Grace"*.

Love in Action

Artist: Daniela Durante-Poetyca

Love in Action is You Being You

    As you live deeper and deeper in Your Heart, you realize you have awakened and remembered there was only one purpose in this physical Life, and that was to find infinite ways to expand Joy, Creativity, Passion and Love. For as you create the reflection of those qualities, those actions help others find those qualities within themselves.

Reflections of Selves

Artist: John Pitre

My Soul Casts Reflections of My Other Selves

Imagine You talking to You from other aspects of Your Being. When the knowingness presents the Truth, one will sit in council and acknowledge the existence that each and every expression of Self is a reflection of an experience to expand the Soul and most importantly The One.

Sacred Contract to Self

© Poetyca

Artist: Daniela Durante-Poetyca

I acknowledge and command my Totality to be in the flow of harmony, balance, love, joy and prosperity in the Allness of Now.

I move and have my Being in the fluidity of change with child-like anticipation and curiosity.

I hold the passion for living and loving with everyone I know and meet.

I live in the wisdom and understanding of compassion and strength.

I communicate this Light and Love of free flowing energy with every thought, word and deed.

I Am at peace within the Heart of my Soul/Spirit.

I Am free to express Light and Love.

I AM.

Self Realization

Artist: Alexandria N. Thompson

To be focused on Self Appreciation enhances the willingness to allow Self Love of the Inner Being to F L O W through every cell of the physical mind and body into a state of Realization. In this state the outer world changes, with everything in it transformed to reflect Love in all expressions.

Stop Telling Your Story of What Hurts

Artist: Richard Homola

STOP Telling Your Story of What Hurts and
START Telling Your Story of What Feels Good

Practice that each and every moment and watch your world change. YOU have the power. YOU have the ability. YOU always have the choice. Gratitude and Appreciation are your Divine Abilities to create the reflection of who You Really Are. It's time to remember.

The Future Self

Artist: Achraf Baznani

Might there be belief systems that are actively keeping one from accessing one's Future Self? Is there a task at hand that requires a solution, that perhaps the Future Self can assist with? In the non-physical vibrational reality, where no time or space exists, lives all the answers and solutions that have been created from one's desires on the Journey of Life. The instant there was an asking, there was a creating of an answer, only to be known when one is in an allowing/receiving state.

The Gentle and Strong Spirit

Artist: Jessica Allain

The Gentle Spirit is Strong – The Strong Spirit is Gentle

Look into Me and see YourSelf-
Reach to have what is Yours.
I give you All that you are-
Receive and create All that I Am.

The Gift

Artist: Shakoor Bukhuth

I give to you understanding - So you will know my Love.

I give to you patience - So you will help me find more.

I give to you recognition - So you may know YourSelf.

I give to you silence - So we may communicate.

I give to you a moment's time - So you may know eternity.

I give to you my Self - So we may know the One.

The Imprint of Our Journey

Artist: Erica Wexler

The Imprint of our Journey can be found in Nature, where Nature's Imprint can be found in Universal Knowledge. These Imprints have their own language that don't use words and when you feel it, you will be changed forever.

Through the Eyes of Spirit

Artist: Endre Balogh

When looking through the eyes of human personality you see only the disconnected version of Self and look in judgement of what "appears" to be "negative".

When looking through the Eyes of Spirit you see the True, Unique and Authentic Self and appreciate the created opportunities to expand.

To Enter Our World

Artist: Jessica Allain

*To enter our world, you must first release all beliefs
that tell you "It's Impossible"*

To enter the world of shadows and fears
To understand desires and birth of tears,
The sound of Silence, Peace and Love
Must be brought to the surface above.

Far below, where the shadows sleep
Are rocks and caves and steps too steep
To carry those who fear to hear
The dragon's breath in their ear.

But for those who have the eyes to see
Will know it's just a part of me
Who has been shown how to tame
The raw emotions that leave some lame.

For those that dare to come inside
Will have to lose their ego pride.
The illusion spreads to those who enter
With no understanding of this venture.

Walk Into YourSelf

Artist: Shirley D. Cross-Taylor

Walk Into YourSelf and You Will Realize the Fear of the Unknown Has Only Been Knowing More About YOU

It is there You will find what an Infinite Being You are with Infinite Expressions of Self - All of which, when shared, leads to more aspects of YourSelf. Open up to share who You are so others can enjoy more of who they are.

We All Exist as One

Artist: Erica Wexler

We All Exist as One Eternal Energy and Have Fragmented Our Infinite Perception to Experience What We Call Physical "Life"

In this fragmentation, we each allow the single expression of All That Is to be A Dance, A Poem, A Song and A Story in our individual, fragmented way to be all woven together in the Tapestry of Life. Within the Essence of Love is Spirit's Story reflecting in the physical world ONE truth: We All Exist As One.

We Are Our Income and Outcome

Artist: Shirley D. Cross-Taylor

When in Alignment With Self, One Feels the Vibrational Harmony of the Flowing and Streaming of Consciousness

Within that Harmony exists Joy, Peace, Passion, Abundance, Love ... Life. When in a state of allowing, there is no lack physically, mentally or emotionally and manifests as Well-Being in the physical world.

Without You

Artist: Mihai Criste

Without You, ALL THAT IS Could Not Know ItSelf

Born as an idea from The One, has within ItSelf all the potential to express and fulfill that Idea. There will never be an end to fulfilling the potential that You, the Idea born from ItSelf expresses. For as you have an idea, you are the Co-Creator giving birth to endless Ideas with potentials fulfilling ItSelf. That is Eternal Life.

Spiritual Warrior and Peace

Artist: Ed Hooijmans

The Spiritual Warrior is Calling Upon Self to Emanate Peace by Laying Down the Sword

The Warrior fights for "freedom" with the mighty sword. The Spiritual Warrior lays down the sword knowing the battle has always been with Self.

Writing My Own Story

I Realize I Am Writing My Own Story by My
Thoughts, Feelings and Focus.

As each page (moment) is written from Love, Joy and Passion, every chapter becomes more exciting, more passionate and more full-filling.

Until the end of my story and I can say
What an Exciting Adventure THAT was!!!

My deepest gratitude for everyone who played a part in my story.

With Great Love,
Sherry

Featured Artists

Achraf Baznani
Surreal Photomanipulation Artist/Photographer, born in Marrakech

Country: Morocco
Website: www.baznani.com

Artist's Title	**Book Page Title**
Confused	Freedom
Life is a Puzzle	Future Self
Another World	Journey of the Soul

Adoreluna (Gabriela Şerban)
Digital Artist focused on bringing to life the most colorful parts of Human Imagination

Country: Romania
Email: adorelunadesigns@gmail.com
Website: adoreluna.deviantart.com/
Facebook: www.facebook.com/adorelunadesigns/

Artist's Title	**Book Page Title**
Ollie's Secret: the Time for Our Favorite Stories	Into the Mystic

---

Alexandria N. Thompson (Alexandria Dior)

Freelance Graphic Designer specializing in Photomanipulation and Mixed Media

Country: United States
Website: www.gothic-fate.com
Other Contact Information: alexandriadior.deviantart.com/

Artist's Title   **Book Page Title**

Witch of Endor   Self Realization

Alla Tsyplakova – AkuBakaArts

Country: Russia
Website: www.deviantart.com/akubakaarts

Artist's Title   **Book Page Title**

Beautiful Despair   Inspiration

Anto Machado (Antoshines)

Artist, Hobbyist, Digital Artist

Country: India
Website: www.deviantart.com/antoshines

Artist's Title   **Book Page Title**

Dreams Mashup   Always Moving Toward Becoming

Benedigital aka Ben Encarnacion

Visionary Mixed Media Artist from Los Angeles, CA

Country: United States – California – Los Angeles
Email: bene@benedigital.com
Facebook: www.facebook.com/benedigitalArts

Artist's Title   **Book Page Title**

Revival   Just Be YourSelf

Daniel B. Holeman

Visionary Artist depicting "Art of Awakening" - uplifting and profound Sacred Imagery

Country: United States
Email: danielholeman@gmail.com
Website: www.AwakenVisions.com

Artist's Title	**Book Page Title**
Earth, Water, Air V043	All is Good in the World
Earth Aura H007	In the World in Which I Travel

Daniela Durante – Poetyca

Poet, Sensitive, and Observer of Nature, combining Poetry and Spirituality in Graphic Design

Country: Italy
Website: poetyca.altervista.org/
Facebook: www.facebook.com/tavolozzadivita/
Blog: poetyca.wordpress.com

Artist's Title	**Book Page Title**
Complice/Accomplice	Love in Action
Eternità/Eternity	Sacred Contract to Self

Ed Hooijmans (ED-Creations)

Artist, Digital Artist

Country: Netherlands
Website: ed-creations.deviantart.com/

Artist's Title	**Book Page Title**
Dreamland	Dream
Only Five Minutes Left	Hocus Pocus
Immortals	Spiritual Warrior and Peace

Endre Balogh

Violinist - Photographer - Digital Fine Artist living in Los Angeles, CA

Country:	United States – California – Los Angeles
Email:	Strad1728@mindspring.com
Website:	endresart.com
Facebook:	www.facebook.com/SacredGeometrybyEndre

Artist's Title	**Book Page Title**
Sacred Geometry 95	Through the Eyes of Spirit

Erica Wexler

Fine Oil Painter and Graphic Designer born and raised in Southern California

Country:	United States – California
Email:	ericawexlerart@gmail.com
Website:	www.EricaWexlerArt.com
Facebook:	www.facebook.com/EricaWexlerArt/

Artist's Title	**Book Page Title**
Manifest	A Heart That is Open
A Beauty in the Ether	Fear of Change
Purging Darkness	Living in Grace
Harmonious Passions	The Imprint of Our Journey
Infinite Reflections	We All Exist as One

Jessica Allain

Self-Taught Digital Artist, specializing in Fantasy and Gothic art, Freelance Book Cover Artist

Country:	Canada – New Brunswick
Email:	Jessicaallainart@hotmail.com
Website:	www.enchanted-whispers.com/
Facebook:	www.facebook.com/EnchantedWhispers

Artist's Title	**Book Page Title**
Fantasy Woman and Horse Art Print	The Gentle and Strong Spirit
Fantasy Little girl Witch child doing magic art print	To Enter Our World

John Pitre

Master of Fantasy and Surrealism, one of the most widely published Artists in modern history

Country: United States – Hawaii – Honolulu
Email: info@pitreart.com
Website: www.johnpitre.com/
Facebook: www.facebook.com/JohnPitreArt/

Artist's Title   **Book Page Title**

Ascension   Reflections of Selves

Koh Sangwoo

Artwork conveys Passion of Emotion in the figures

Country: Korea – now lives and works in New York, New York, United States
Email: KohSangwoo@yahoo.com
Website: www.kohsangwoo.com/
Facebook: www.facebook.com/koh.sangwoo

Artist's Title   **Book Page Title**

When Sun Is In Love (English translation)   I Am Feeling Joy

Mariusz Lewandowski

Surrealist Artist in Gorowo Iławeckie, Olsztyn, Poland

Country: Poland – Olsztyn – Gorowo Iławeckie
Email: inter-art@o2.pl
Website: www.mariuszlewandowski.pl/
Facebook: www.facebook.com/MalarstwoNowoczesneLewandowski/

Artist's Title   **Book Page Title**

SoulHunter (English translation)   Karma is Self Image

Mihai Criste (Mihai2000)
Creative Romanian Surrealist Artist

Country:	Romania
Email:	mihai82000@yahoo.com
Website:	http://www.mihaicriste.blogspot.com

Artist's Title

Rien ne se perd, tout se transforme, 2011, oil on canvas, 80/120 cm

Book Page Title

Without You

Misticos Online (José Augusto)

Country:	Brazil
E-mail:	misticosonline.joseaugusto@hotmail.com
Website:	www.misticosonline.com.br
Facebook:	www.facebook.com/misticosonline/
Other Contact Information:	+55 11 4850-8458 Direct Phone Number

Artist's Title

Book Page Title

Birth to Self

Richard Homola
Freelance Digital Artist

Country:	Czech Republic
Email:	richard.homola@gmail.com
Website:	www.richardhomola.com

Artist's Title

Excalibur

Book Page Title

Stop Telling Your Story of What Hurts

Shakoor Bukhuth (aka Shaun Beyond)
Multidisciplinary Designer and Illustrator, as well as Explorer and Creator

Country:	Mauritius
Email:	shakoorbukhuth@gmail.com
Website:	www.instagram.com/shaunbeyond/
	www.behance.net/Shakoor_Bukhuth
Facebook:	www.facebook.com/shaunbeyond/

Artist's Title	**Book Page Title**
Alter-Natives	The Gift

Shirley B. Cross-Taylor
Photographer and Digital Photomanipulation Artist currently living in Oregon

Country:	United States – Oregon
Email:	treasureprints@msn.com
Website:	www.imageopolis.com/photographer.asp?id=75004#.WyGT8fUnZLM
Facebook:	www.facebook.com/shirley.d.cross

Artist's Image Title	**Book Page Title**
The Guardian Blue Eyes	Animal Spirit Guides
Aethereal Waterfall	Conversation with Your Heart
Listen to the Music	Dear Self
Birth of a Naiad	Language of Love
Summer Wind	Walk Into YourSelf
Dreaming Soul	We Are Our Income and Outcome

About the Author

Through years of healing work, Sherry Richardson has been inspired by Spirit to share a different way of looking at "reality".

Within the framework of healing, her journey has offered her the ability to share with others the simplicity of powerful words that resonate with the nature of the Human Spirit.

She has come to realize that the moment the "thinking mind" changes to a different way of perceiving "reality", a shift takes place.

Printed in the United States
By Bookmasters